W9-CZV-292

LIGHT

Troll Associates

LIGHT

by Rae Bains

Illustrated by Chuck Harriton

Troll Associates

Library of Congress Cataloging in Publication Data

Bains, Rae.
 Light.

 Summary: Explains the importance of light, without
which plants and trees could not live, the wind would
not blow, and the earth would become a dead lump of
rock and ice.
 1. Light—Juvenile literature. [1. Light]
I. Harriton, Chuck, ill. II. Title.
QC360.B35   1984   535   84-2719
ISBN 0-8167-0202-0 (lib. bdg.)
ISBN 0-8167-0203-9 (pbk.)

Can you imagine what the world would be like without light? It would be totally dark all the time. People would stumble around, unable to see. Our eyes would be useless. Plants and trees would soon die, because they need light to stay alive.

Green plants use the energy of sunlight to change water and carbon dioxide into food. Plants cannot live where it is dark all the time. If there were no plants, all the animals on Earth would die. That's because plants become food for animals. And these animals become food for other animals.

This is called the *food chain*. Plants are the first link in the food chain. Without light, plants could not grow, so the food chain would not begin. And before long, all life would vanish from the Earth.

Without light, the wind would stop blowing. Wind is simply air that is moving because of changes in temperature. And these changes of temperature are caused by sunlight. If there were no sunlight, the temperature would never change. The world would be cold all the time.

Then all the water on Earth would stop flowing and start to freeze. There would be no rain and no snow. The planet Earth would become a dead lump of rock and ice.

But we don't have to worry about these things. Every day our world glows with life because it receives plenty of light. The Earth's main source of natural light is the sun. It warms the Earth. It pours energy into every living thing. The energy in sunlight keeps our world alive and healthy.

Sunlight and all other kinds of light move very fast. When you raise your window shade in the morning, the sunlight seems to pour in at once. But it takes about eight minutes for a ray of sunlight to travel all the way from the sun to the Earth.

Traveling at exactly the same speed—the speed of light—it takes much longer for light to reach us from the stars. That's because the stars are farther away from us than the sun is.

The light from the star that is closest to our solar system takes about four years to reach Earth! That distance is so great that we measure it in *light-years* instead of in miles or kilometers. A light-year is the distance light travels in one year.

Although we can see the light from stars twinkling in the night sky, this light does not have any real effect on our world. But the light from our sun does affect us. The sunlight that bathes Earth is made of different kinds of rays.

Two important kinds are infrared rays and ultraviolet rays. If you sit in the sun, your body takes in infrared rays. Infrared rays are invisible heat rays. That's why you feel warm when you're out in the sunshine.

Ultraviolet rays are also invisible. You cannot feel the sun's ultraviolet rays, but you can feel what they do to you. It is because of these rays that people get a suntan or a sunburn.

Ultraviolet rays can be very dangerous if you stay out in them too long. Ultraviolet rays reach us even when the day is cloudy and cool. And people can get sunburned then, too. Still, we *do* need small amounts of ultraviolet rays. They help our bodies make vitamin D, which we use to build strong bones and teeth.

The sun sends out many ultraviolet rays that do not reach Earth. They don't all reach us because there is a shield around our planet. That shield is our atmosphere. In outer space, there is no atmosphere. That's why astronauts traveling through space must wear special clothing to protect themselves against ultraviolet rays.

Infrared and ultraviolet rays are invisible rays of sunlight. But the rays of sunlight that we can see are called visible light. The visible light from the sun appears to be white. But it is really made up of all colors. When it passes through a glass prism, something strange happens. The light is broken up into a rainbowlike band of colors—from red, orange, and yellow...to green, blue, and violet.

This is called the spectrum of visible light. Sometimes raindrops act like a prism, breaking sunlight into the different colors we call a rainbow.

All together, the different kinds of rays that radiate from the sun make up Earth's main source of natural light. Other kinds of light we use come from artificial sources, like candles, electric light bulbs, oil lamps, and burning matches. All of these sources of artificial light are made by people.

The most powerful artificial light comes from a *laser*. A laser is a machine that produces a narrow beam of light that has a single color. The energy of laser light is used to do many wonderful things. Surgeons use it to perform delicate operations on eyes, blood vessels, and other parts of the body. Laser beams are also used in many industries and by scientists in laboratories.

Light, whether it is natural or artificial, travels in a straight line. If nothing stops a ray of light, it will continue traveling on and on in the same line. But in our world, light is always being stopped by one thing or another.

What happens to light when it hits something? That depends on what it hits. When

light hits a smooth, shiny surface, it is reflected. A mirror, a calm lake, the silvery metal on a kitchen toaster—all these are surfaces that reflect light.

Sometimes light is turned from its straight line. When this happens, we say that the light is refracted, or bent. When you stand a pencil in a glass of water, it looks as if the pencil is bent where it enters the water. That is because the light rays have been refracted by the water.

We often use lenses to refract light so we can see things more clearly. You are probably familiar with eyeglass lenses, telescope lenses, microscope lenses, and magnifying-glass lenses. Each of these lenses refracts light, or bends it in a certain way.

Sometimes, when light hits an object, some of the light stays there. When this happens, we say the light is absorbed. The darker an object is, the more light it will absorb, or take in.

You may have heard that you will feel cooler on hot, sunny days if you wear white clothing. That's true. A dark shirt takes in light energy and holds it, making you warm. A white shirt takes in a lot less light energy, so you will not feel as warm. What happens to the light energy that is not absorbed? It is reflected away from the white shirt.

When light hits a surface and can't pass through, the surface is said to be *opaque*. A book, a wall, a rock, and your body are all opaque.

When light passes through something but we cannot see clearly through that thing, we say it is *translucent*. Frosted glass, fog, and most lamp shades are translucent.

When light passes right through something and we can also see right through that thing, we say it is *transparent*. A pane of clear glass is transparent. So are clear water and the air around us.

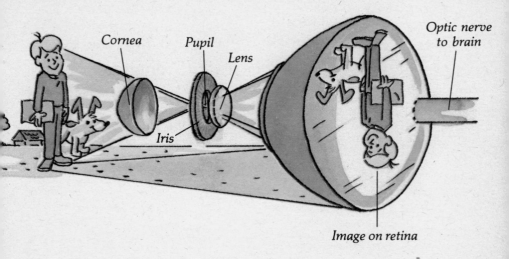

Cornea
Pupil
Lens
Iris
Optic nerve to brain
Image on retina

The outer covering of your eye is also transparent. What happens when light reaches your eye? First, it passes through the transparent outer covering of the eye, called the *cornea*. Then the light passes through the *lens*, which is also transparent.

The lens focuses and refracts, or bends, the light. The image of what the eye is seeing forms on the back lining of the eye. This lining is opaque. It is called the *retina*. Finally, the information of what is being seen is carried to the brain.

A camera works very much like the eye. It takes in light, focuses it through the lens, and forms an image on a surface that reacts to light. This surface is called photographic film.

Photographic film has a chemical on it. This chemical is changed by light. Where a great deal of light hits the film, the chemical changes a lot. Where less light hits the film, there is less chemical change. These chemical changes cause the dark and light patterns that make photographs and motion pictures.

Light also affects the chemicals in paints and dyes. The coloring of a chair cushion that gets a lot of sunlight may fade after a while. The paint on the sunny sides of a house may also fade because of light shining on it.

Light affects us every second of our lives. It brightens our day. It helps grow the food we eat. It helps keep us warm and healthy. It gives us movies and moonbeams and all the colors of the rainbow. And it makes it possible for us to see all the beauty of the world we live in.